How to Patent an Idea or Invention

An Easy-To-Read Guide for the Process of Getting a Patent or 'Patent Pending' Provisional Patent

~ How to Get a Patent ~

By J.P. Schafer

Table of Contents

Introduction 1

Chapter 1: When to Patent (and When NOT to Tell People About It) 7

Chapter 2: Where to Go and What to Do 13

Chapter 3: Getting Help and Avoiding Scams 17

Chapter 4: Being Unique is Good, But Not Critical 25

Chapter 5: Get Ready to Sweat 29

Chapter 5: Moving from a Provisional to a Full Patent and Understanding Terms and Fees 35

Conclusions 39

Introduction

So you've got the next breakthrough invention! With your new idea that's poised to take the market by storm, you don't want anyone beating you to the punch. Nor do you want any tag-along imitators or giant corporations claiming your idea as their own. It's *your* idea, and *you* want to retain full ownership of it, so you'd like to know a thing or two about patenting.

A patent is a temporary government-issued monopoly that prevents others from making, using or selling your product. Holding a patent on an invention grants you the authority to issue licenses to others (individuals or companies) who want to make and sell your product.

You made the right decision by getting this book, because for a process this involved (and at times, complicated), you want to have a good fundamental understanding of the process before you start making decisions on how to proceed. If you're invention is a good one, then you're off to a good start, but 95% of the success you will have hinges on how you go about procuring your patent and finding partners to help you make and sell your product. Every industry operates differently. You will need to figure out which industry your patent fits into and who the major players are in that industry.

This book will help you better understand the patenting process and will provide step-by-step instructions on the how, when, and where of patenting.

4

© Copyright 2014 by LCPublifish LLC - All rights reserved.

This document is geared towards providing reliable information in regards to the topic and issue covered. The publication is sold with the idea that the publisher is not required to render accounting, officially permitted, or otherwise, qualified services. If advice is necessary, legal or professional, a practiced individual in the profession should be ordered.

- From a Declaration of Principles which was accepted and approved equally by a Committee of the American Bar Association and a Committee of Publishers and Associations.

In no way is it legal to reproduce, duplicate, or transmit any part of this document in either electronic means or in printed format. Recording of this publication is strictly prohibited and any storage of this document is not allowed unless with written permission from the publisher. All rights reserved.

The information provided herein is stated to be truthful and consistent, in that any liability, in terms of inattention or otherwise, by any usage or abuse of any policies, processes, or directions contained within is solely and completely the responsibility of the recipient reader. Under no circumstances will any legal responsibility or blame be held against the publisher for any reparation, damages, or monetary loss due to the information herein, either directly or indirectly.

Respective authors own all copyrights not held by the publisher.

The information herein is offered for informational purposes solely, and is universal as so. The presentation of the information is without contract or any type of guarantee assurance.

The trademarks that are used are without any consent, and the publication of the trademark is without permission or backing by the trademark owner. All trademarks and brands within this book are for clarifying purposes only and are the owned by the owners themselves, not affiliated with this document.

Chapter 1: When to Patent (and When NOT to Tell People About It)

In the United States, if you've applied for a patent and have marked your product thus: "patent pending," you still do not have any formal legal protection that prevents others from producing or selling your product. Phrases like "patent pending" or "patent applied for" don't have real legal effect. They simply give the market a heads-up to the fact that an application for a patent has been filed.

In the world of patenting, it's important to know where you stand. You must be very careful about giving out inaccurate information about your product's status. You can only label your product as "patented" or tell people it's patented after your full patent application has been submitted and approved. Claiming a patent prematurely is against the law and could result in serious repercussion.

The first step for many in inventors is the filing of a "provisional patent," which essentially provides a formal recognition of the date in which the inventor first sought patent protection. You can convert your provisional patent into a full patent application at any time within one year of filing your provisional patent.

Taking advantage of the "provisional patent" option prevents people from being priced out of the patent game by giving them a low-cost placeholder for their idea or invention while they explore the true market potential for their idea.

A provisional patent allows you to get a date on file with the patent office. The patent game is first come first serve. You must get something on record as early as possible and a provisional patent is a great way to do this. If you're in doubt about whether to pursue your provisional patent, remember that the law in the United States currently holds that the *first to file* for a patent is the legal owner of any product or idea. Even if you can prove that you invented a product before someone else filed for a patent, the person who filed first will still be the legal owner of the invention.

You're free to pursue your patent before you have an actual prototype of the invention. All you need is the ability to demonstrate (even on paper) what your invention is and how it can be used. When you're creating your drawing, illustration, or 3D rendering of your prospective invention, you should already be considering what you're going to need to capture the attention of a prospective licensee.

A licensee is a person or company whom you will give authorization to manufacture and distribute your product after you've patented it. You're going to want to produce a rendering that looks interesting and exciting. You're also going to want to produce something that clearly demonstrates some kind of problem-solving capability. Remember, a patent alone doesn't make you any money, your invention has to find its own way into the market.

A natural question you probably have at this point is whether you should have a licensee ready to go before you invest in procuring the patent. This is a tricky question to assess and there is no right answer, as the process can enfold in a multitude of ways. There are devoted licensing firms that will help you mediate this process. So depending on how clandestine you want to be (how protective over your invention) you may want to reach out to a licensing firm, such as Lambert and Lambert, as your first step.

What's important to consider when determining your sequence of action, is that your licensee will ultimately determine whether or not you're going to make any money. If you don't have a good licensee on board with a good strategy then you're going to have trouble. That said, you have essentially no protection for your invention before you secure your patent. The one exception would be if you have your licensee, or any other interested party, sign a confidentiality agreement. But even with the agreement signed and in place, it would only protect you from infringement by the specific parties with whom you signed the agreement. Often engineering firms and licensing firms will sign confidentiality agreements. Investing firms typically will not sign agreements though. Investing firms are presumably receiving a multitude of different investment ideas. If an investment firm signed confidentiality agreements with two parties who happened to be representing similar inventions, then they would face a potential liability issue.

To keep things simple, here's a step-by-step recommended course of action. Remember though, every situation is different, so make sure you study the legal norms and processes of patenting thoroughly as you make your decisions on how to proceed:

Step One: Put together a detailed rendering of your invention by drawing it or illustrating it electronically.

Step Two: Assess how and where your product could be optimally marketed and investigate licensees with whom you'd like to work with for the purposes of production and distribution.

Step Three: Now that you have a clearer idea of what your invention is and how and through whom it could be marketed, go ahead and apply for a provisional patent. This will attach your name and rights to the idea and give you something more substantial to present to prospective licensees. With provisional patent applications, it's better to file sooner rather than later, so get this in immediately so you'll have some reasonable and intelligible documented concept of your invention on record.

Step Four: Approach licensees with your idea. By this point you should have very detailed and clear renderings of your idea, how it's to be manufactured, which materials etc.

Step Five: Apply for your full patent. Before your idea goes into production you will want to have your full patent in-hand so that your rights to the proceeds of your invention are fully protected.

Chapter 2: Where to Go and What to Do

Provisional and full patents can be applied for through the United States Patent and Trademark Office (USPTO). On their website at http://www.uspto.gov/ you will be able to download the necessary applications for various patent types.

You will need to know what type of patent you are applying for, as they come in a few different varieties.

Utility Patents:

Got a new gadget or device that's going to make life easier? Time to get a utility patent. Utility patents are by far the most common type of patent issued by the USPTO. Approximately 90% of all patents issued are utility patents.

US law is careful to codify that all inventions receiving a utility patent must be "capable of use." This provision is to prevent people from attempting to patent time machines or other fantastical inventions that cannot demonstrate a clear usability and/or utility. There are a series of thresholds that must be met in order to successfully obtain a utility patent. The invention must come with a clear description on how it is operated. The invention must have some beneficial utility, in other words you can't patent something that's clearly nefarious in intent. Finally the invention must be practical, having some real world application and integrative capacity with everyday life. If an invention falls short in any of these areas, then its utility patent application may be rejected.

Design Patents:

Design patents safeguard the owner's right to assert claim on a specific ornamental design. This patent would apply to the design of objects such as furniture, jewelry, computer icons or fonts, and beverage containers. Design patents are distinct from trademarks, which are intended primarily to help protect consumers from brand imitators.

Plant Patents:

As the name states, plant patents protect a party's claim to the cultivation, use, and sale of a specific strain of plant.

Reissue Patent:

Reissue patents are issued to correct some element that was omitted or made in error in a previous patent.

Chapter 3: Getting Help and Avoiding Scams

Daytime television is swarming with ads for prospective inventors. But how do you avoid the scams and determine who can really help you?

Invention submission companies usually offer to research your invention, get you started with the patent submission process, and help you make contact with relevant industry licensees. Unfortunately, these companies have earned a sullied reputation after being subject to millions of dollars worth of fraud claims.

Fortunately, picking out the scams from the legitimate sources of support is not that difficult. Good invention submission companies will not ask for a lot of money up front, because they are generating adequate funds from their portion of royalties from successful inventions. Suspect companies will often ask you for a lot of money up front, usually a few hundred dollars to start. They will use this money to create a market report for you and then ask you to invest another several thousand to help you initiate your patenting and licensing process.

A good way to screen out suspect invention submission companies is to ask for a full disclosure of fees up front. Ask them to clarify their fee structure from the initial consultation, to the research, all the way to the submission of a quality full patent application. If this expense seems unreasonable, then it's probably because the company in question has a poor track record in successfully helping their inventors bring their products to market.

The American Inventors Protection Act, established in 1999, vamped up protections for inventors by requiring invention submission companies to disclose the following information about their last five years of business:

- How many inventions the company has evaluated

- The company's total number of customers

- How many of the customers realized a net profit from the services of the company, meaning that the inventor made more money from the marketing and sale of the invention than they paid to the firm

- How many of the company's inventors ended up licensing their products thanks to the company's involvement.

Request this information from any company you're considering working with, and simply make a good common sense evaluation of whether or not this company's reputation is worth your time and money. Remember, you have other options for getting help, such as patent agents and patent attorneys.

The USPTO advises enrolling the assistance of a patent attorney before proceeding with your application. Patent attorneys usually have a combination of both technical and legal expertise. Many of them are practiced engineers, biologists, chemists, botanists etc. who have been drawn to the field of patent law.

When investigating a potential patent attorney, be sure to search for someone who has the required knowledge to suit your invention's technical category. For example, if you are inventing a new vaccine, then a patent attorney with an MD or biology degree is your best choice. Many patent attorneys have direct experience working for the USPTO and can thus leverage their useful "inside" knowledge on your behalf.

Relative to invention submission companies, the patent attorney profession isn't plagued with corruption and general sketchiness. You will, of course, get a few bad apples who will try to make a quick buck by filing for patents that they know to be essentially worthless.

Here are a few things to consider when evaluating patent attorneys.

- Does the attorney delegate the patent search to a professional searcher or does she conduct the search on her own? Usually the best patent attorneys will delegate their patent search to a professional searcher.

- Will the attorney provide a "presentability opinion" in writing? A "presentability opinion" is a document that compares your invention with similar ones in the marketplace and explains how your invention could potentially be asserted as unique, and thus patentable.

- Is the attorney charging a price per hour that you can afford? Usually solo practicing attorneys will be less expensive than larger firms.

There are a few ways you can go about locating prospective patent attorneys. The USPTO website has a listing of patent attorneys by state. Another idea is to join an inventors club or MeetUp group in your area and ask for a recommendation.

Another potentially valuable human resource is a "Patent Agent." A patent agent has passed the USPTO's Patent Bar and can be hired by inventors to represent their interests during the course of the patenting process.

Early on in your process, while you are researching ideas that are similar to your own, having a patent agent on hand to help you search is a good practice. "The search" is a part of the invention process that many inventors dread, because it involves facing the prospect that your unique idea may not be so unique after all. In actuality, finding inventions on the market that are similar to your own idea is a good thing. We'll talk more about that in the following chapter.

You may be able to use the internet or other research methods to find a few products similar to your own. A patent agent can conduct a much more thorough search through the records of the USPTO.

They say an author should never design his or her own book cover. A similar principle applies to inventors. Generally, you should avoid conducting your own search through the USPTO. A good search requires a very level-headed and unattached evaluation and whoever conducts the search should have minimal attachment to the prospective invention.

Chapter 4: Being Unique is Good, But Not Critical

Many prospective inventors make the mistake of dismissing their idea once a google search turns up a similar product or product(s). If you find similar products, then you are actually finding proof that your invention has an existing place in the market. Someone has already, presumably, gone through the process of bringing a form of your idea to market and is perhaps having some luck with it. This doesn't mean that your version of the idea is not still uniquely patentable and can be used to service a broader market, or more specific niche market.

Usually you will be able to find a way in which your design is uniquely better or different than what currently exists on the marketplace. As you begin to understand your invention's unique elements, you should parlay this analysis into a bit of business planning. If you're serious about making money off of your invention than you're going to have to find someone who will manufacture it and sell it.

The person(s) who've already "invented" your idea can actually help you kick start your market research. See if you can't acquire some idea as to where their version of your invention is being deployed, what countries, states, online sites etc. Do you believe that your version of the product can generate a lot more attention and revenue? Can you articulate this to a manufacturer, distributor and/or licensee? If you can find a market for your product, then you should also be able to find a way to patent your *specific* version of the product.

Here's an interesting factoid: Thomas Edison wasn't actually the first person to patent the light bulb. Someone beat him to the punch by two years. The reason Edison gets all the recognition from this invention is because he was the first person to come up with a method to consistently attach the white-hot filament to the bulb and to ensure uniform diameter of the filament.

If you're truly inspired by your invention, then you will find in most cases, that even if someone has had thoughts (and even taken action) along similar lines, you probably do have something that in some way is truly unique.

Chapter 5: Get Ready to Sweat

As soon as you file your provisional patent you're given one year to file for the complete patent before losing your filing status. This is going to be a busy year for you as you attempt to find ways to further crystallize your patent claim while bringing partner parties to the table to help you make and sell your product.

Your initial expense for filing your patent (provisional or otherwise) is going to be about $350. This doesn't include any fees owed to your attorney, patent agent, or any other third party. While you wait for your invention to be approved, you will need to get to work on a few other tasks. Here are a few things you can do to help you best position your invention for the market.

Put together a working prototype

Venture capitalists and licensees are going to be a lot more interested in something if they can actually try it out before deciding whether they want to invest in it. Having a few prototypes made for your invention will allow you to use it on your own and address concerns and consider improvements.

Conduct market research

Put together a survey on Google Surveys or elsewhere to gage who's interested in your product. Figure out who and where your customers are, and you'll be well equipped to lead an outstanding marketing effort.

Conduct market trials and get feedback

Send out some prototypes to a carefully selected test demographic. Let them use the product for a few weeks and report back their findings. Remember to ask them if this is something they'd pay money to have and how much.

Get a high profile endorsement

Do you know someone with a huge twitter or youtube following who would really enjoy your product? See if you can get them a working prototype in exchange for some added publicity.

When it comes to approaching potential manufacturing and distributing partners, avoid larger companies. For example, you wouldn't want to ask Johnson and Johnson to make and distribute your patented shampoo. Larger companies tend to have their own Research and Development departments where they conduct their own innovation and inventing. Usually they will not take meetings with entrepreneurial level inventors, because they risk encountering a product similar to one they've already got in research and development, at which point you could potentially bring legal action against the company for making and selling the product you pitched to them.

Companies that you should consider approaching include new product development companies, marketing agencies, and business planning consultants.

A new product developer is a specialist who can assist with many aspects of the invention to market process. New product developers are essentially analysts and networkers in their industry capable of spotting important market trends and recognizing which individuals and corporations are ideally positioned to exploit them. New product developers can help you find prototypers and general manufacturers. They can also help you find capital and good legal help. The hourly rates for new product developers are usually at least $100 and because you have to work with them for several months, they can run a pretty steep tab. This time can be shortened some if you've already made a lot of progress on your own.

A market research firm does just that. They uncover the potential market for your product and assess its ability to compete worldwide. Most market research firms are not going to take on a new product for any less than five thousand and if your invention foray is in a particularly research intensive field (like pharmaceuticals), then you could be facing a tab upwards of fifty thousand. If you have the time, you may want to attempt the market research on your own. You can do this by conducting research online and by visiting trade shows. You will also want to acquaint yourself (and your potential investors/partners) with key metrics such as the overall size of the market and the typical margins of the industry, as well as the standard royalty rates.

A business planning consultant will write a business plan for you and help you determine whether you're ultimately going to get paid for all this hard work.

They will make that determination for you by helping you develop accurate financial forecasts that account for your product sales, royalties, and expense. As with your patent attorney, your business consultant needs to be intimately familiar with the industry and niche your product fits into. Prepare to be billed $100 an hour to work with an experienced business consultant.

Need some shortcuts to save a few bucks? Try academia. Your local business school may have some opportunities for you. You could offer to make a donation to the college in exchange for some market research, or you can pay the students to help you. This route will cost you much less than $100 an hour.

Chapter 5: Moving from a Provisional to a Full Patent and Understanding Terms and Fees

When you file for a full patent after filing for a provisional patent, the filing date of the provisional patent will be recorded as the date of invention. You can convert to a full patent by following one of two routes:

- Filing a full patent application that claims the provisional application's filing date.

- Filing a petition to convert the provisional application into a Non-Provisional Application, along with all materials required to do so.

(According to the United States Patent and Trademark Office, USPTO)

The difference between these two options is the resulting overall patent term. With the first option, the term will be measured from the filing date of the Provisional application. With the second option, the term will be measured from the filing date of your Non-Provisional application.

It's important to take note of terms, because the time in which your invention is protected by a patent is fixed. Utility patents expire after 20 years and require the payment of "Patent Maintenance Fees." After having your patent on file for 3.5 years you will be assessed a fee upwards of two thousand dollars. After it's been on file for 7.5 years you will be assessed a fee upwards of five thousand dollars, and after 11.5 years, you will be assessed a fee of more than ten thousand dollars. You will need to pay these fees if you want your invention to remain protected by the USPTO. It's expected, obviously, that your invention will be making money and the USPTO does not want people to squat on a patent that someone else could be using productively.

In order to successfully use your Provisional filing date for your Non Provisional patent, you will have to show that the two applications (your Provisional and Non Provisional applications) are roughly similar, ie that they're both representing the same invention. You may have made some tweaks over the last year, and that's fine and expected, but your Non Provisional product should have a very clear connection to the product described in your Provisional patent. To ensure you can make this connection persuasively, the USPT recommends using very detailed and high-quality illustrations for your provisional application. Remember filing a provisional application does not guarantee that you will get a patent. The USPTO doesn't even evaluate these applications. It is just a place marker; and in order to take full advantage of this place marker, you need to make sure that your non provisional application is thorough and showing a clear semblance to the provisional application.

Conclusions

It's important that you do your research and spend a lot of time thinking and strategizing before pursuing a patent. It is said that only 60% of patent applications earn approval from the USPTO and among these issued patents only 20% are ever commercialized. And less than 50% of the commercialized patents ever return a net profit for the inventor, recouping the cost of the patent attorneys, filing fees and other expenses. That's 50% of 20% of 60%, which equates to only a total of 5% of patent applications that end up actually making money for their inventors.

Though the strength of your original idea is certainly important, the reality is that a person who follows a better patenting process and brings a mediocre idea to market will fare better than a person who follows a poorer process with a fantastic idea. The key things to know:

- Get your provisional patent filed as soon as possible! This will be your placeholder to ensure no one can claim original ownership over your idea.

- Be highly selective in who you enroll to assist you in the process. You have a lot of options at varying expense levels. Regardless of how much you're going to invest in getting help, try and find people who have familiarity with your product's relevant industry.

- If you are considering an Invention Submission company ask them to disclose their full fee structure up front and demand that they provide their business data per the dictates of the 1999 American Inventors Protection Act.

- Get ready to roll up your sleeves and get to work. You can't just patent an idea and walk away expecting to get rich. You have exactly one year after you file for your provisional patent to complete the process for a full patent. During this time you need to also set up a viable production and distribution infrastructure for your product.

- Make sure a clear connection can be drawn connecting your Provisional patent to your Full (Non Provisional) Patent, as this will ensure that you retain the earlier filing date of record.

Good luck! And happy inventing!

Finally, I'd like to thank you for purchasing this book! If you enjoyed it or found it helpful, I'd greatly appreciate it if you'd take a moment to leave a review on Amazon. Thank you!

Made in the USA
Las Vegas, NV
02 December 2024